SPOTLIGHT ON NATURE
EAGLE
MELISSA GISH

CREATIVE EDUCATION · CREATIVE PAPERBACKS

Published by Creative Education and Creative Paperbacks
P.O. Box 227, Mankato, Minnesota 56002
Creative Education and Creative Paperbacks are imprints
of The Creative Company
www.thecreativecompany.us

Design by Chelsey Luther; production by Colin O'Dea
Art direction by Rita Marshall
Printed in the United States of America

Photographs by Alamy (BIOSPHOTO, blickwinkel, Danita Delimont
Creative, Design Pics Inc, David Gowans, JamesBrey, ZUMA Press, Inc.),
Creative Commons Wikimedia (Murray Foubister/Flickr, Andy Morffew
/Flickr, Shreeram M V), iStockphoto (ca2hill, jaypetersen, KatPaws, Miki
Meller, Mfotophile, outlook, predrag1, undefined undefined), Minden
Pictures (Suzi Eszterhas, Alan Murphy/BIA, Luis Quinta/NPL, Michael
Quinton), Shutterstock (AndreAnita)

Library of Congress Cataloging-in-Publication Data
Names: Gish, Melissa, author.
Title: Eagle / Melissa Gish.
Series: Spotlight on nature.
Includes index.
Summary: A detailed chronology of developmental milestones drives this life
study of eagles, including their habitats, physical features, and conservation
measures taken to protect these birds of prey.
Identifiers: LCCN 2018041786 / ISBN 978-1-64026-181-5 (hardcover) /
ISBN 978-1-62832-744-1 (pbk) / ISBN 978-1-64000-299-9 (eBook)
Subjects: LCSH: Eagles—Juvenile literature. / Eagles—Habitat—Juvenile
literature. / Eagles—Conservation—Juvenile literature.
Classification: LCC QL696.F32 G568 2019 / DDC 598.9/42—dc23

First Edition HC 9 8 7 6 5 4 3 2 1
First Edition PBK 9 8 7 6 5 4 3 2 1

CONTENTS

MEET THE FAMILY
Bald Eagles of
Anticosti Island   4

LIFE BEGINS   7

Featured Family
Welcome to the World   8
First Meal   10

**EARLY
ADVENTURES**   13

Featured Family
Look Who's Crawling   14
Give It a Try   16

LIFE LESSONS   19

Featured Family
This Is How It's Done   20
Practice Makes Perfect   22

**EAGLE
SPOTTING**   25

Family Album Snapshots   28
Words to Know   30
Learn More   31
Index   32

BALD EAGLES
of Anticosti Island

Anticosti is an island off the coast of Quebec in the Gulf of St. Lawrence. Grey and harbor seals patrol the rocky shores. Deer, moose, snowshoe hares, and lynx roam the forests. High in the branches of a balsam fir tree, a pair of bald eagles has built a nest. Eagle nests are called aeries. The nest is almost as wide as a king-size bed. In the center of the nest are two eggs, each nearly as big as a baseball.

It is late April and only 40 °F (4.4 °C). For the past 35 days, the parents have taken turns sitting on the eggs. This has kept them warm. Inside the eggs, baby bald eagles have been developing. Now, sounds are coming from the eggs. The parents lean their faces close to the eggs, listening intently. Soft cheeping emanates from inside the eggs. It is time for the baby eagles to enter the world.

CLOSE-UP
Brood patch

A brood patch is the bare skin that develops on a bird's breast so the parent can keep its eggs warm. Blood vessels in the featherless skin have more direct contact with the eggs.

CHAPTER ONE

LIFE BEGINS

Eagles are birds of prey, also called raptors. Eagles eat meat and hunt just about any kind of animal they can carry, including snakes, rodents, rabbits, and other birds. Some also hunt monkeys and sloths. Others feed mainly on fish. There are 60 different species of eagle. Eagles live everywhere on Earth except Antarctica, inhabiting mountains, forests, grasslands, and deserts. Eagles are considered apex predators. This means they are found at the top of the food chain. By hunting, they keep smaller animals from overpopulating. They also clean up their habitats by eating the remains of dead animals. Eagles help maintain a natural, healthy balance for all the living things in their habitat.

ANTICOSTI ISLAND BALD EAGLE MILESTONES

DAY 1

 Hatch from the egg
Covered with soft, fluffy feathers called down
Weight: 6 ounces (170 g)

FEATURED FAMILY

Welcome to the World

In the nest on Anticosti Island, the first baby bald eagle pushes against its shell. There is a scraping crack. The egg wobbles. Another scrape. Then silence. The baby is exhausted and must rest. Two hours later, another scrape. The hatchling succeeds in making a pinhole-sized opening in the shell. This is called pipping. The struggle continues for 20 more hours before the first hatchling, a female, finally breaks free. The second, a male, emerges a day later, joining his sibling under their mother's warm wing.

Adult eagles have no natural enemies except for larger eagles. Baby eagles—called nestlings, hatchlings, or eaglets— are vulnerable to a variety of predators. Raccoons, horned owls, hawks, and even other eagles may steal small eaglets from a nest. Eagle parents must closely guard their offspring for their first months of life. Adult eagles use their sharp beaks and talons as weapons. When walking in the nest, parents ball their talons up into fists. This prevents accidental stabbing of their offspring.

Despite also having sharp beaks, eagle hatchlings cannot feed themselves. They cannot even hold up their heads for the first two weeks of life. Hatchlings arrive in the world practically naked

CLOSE-UP
Body temperature

The body temperature of most eagles is about 106 °F (41.1 °C). With enough food for energy, parents can keep their hatchlings warm during cold weather.

② WEEKS

- Able to hold up their heads
- Weight: 1.5 pounds (0.7 kg)

③ WEEKS

- Covered with a secondary coat of down
- Legs turn yellow
- Height: 12 inches (30.5 cm)
- Weight: 2.5 pounds (1.1 kg)

and totally blind. A thin layer of fuzzy feathers called down covers their bony bodies. Their huge eyes partially open within a few hours of hatching, but their vision remains poor for a couple of weeks. Hatchlings cannot regulate their body temperature. Left unprotected, they can get cold and quickly perish. They rely on their mother to keep them warm. They cheep incessantly. She tucks them under her breast and wings.

Gape flange

The fleshy hinge that holds the top and bottom parts of a bird's beak together is called the gape flange. The inside of a bird's mouth is called the gape. Baby eagles have bright yellow or pink gapes. They serve as targets for parents to aim food delivery.

— FEATURED FAMILY —

First Meal

Lying on their sides, the hatchlings look like two balls of whitish-gray fuzz. The father eagle has arrived at the nest with a snowshoe hare carcass. Both parents dig into the meal. They gently place bits of soft tissue in the hatchlings' beaks, one at a time. The hatchlings gulp down the food whole. Then, their bellies full, the mother and her hatchlings settle in for sleep, while the father guards the nest.

(4) **WEEKS**

▸ Legs can support body weight
▸ Crawl around the nest
▸ Weight: 3.5 pounds (1.6 kg)

CLOSE-UP
Patrols

Nesting eagles keep other raptors away from their nests by patrolling one to two square miles (2.6–5.2 sq km) around the nest site.

CHAPTER TWO

EARLY ADVENTURES

Nesting eagles brood, or sit on their eggs, for one to two months, depending on the species. Most eagle species have one to three offspring. South America's endangered Chaco eagle lays just one egg each October. Other species, such as golden eagles, may lay four eggs. When eagle hatchlings are about four weeks old, they become eaglets. The more offspring a pair of eagles has, the greater the risk that not all will survive. This is because eaglets fight over food. Weaker eaglets may starve to death or get pushed out of the nest. This is called siblicide and is common among birds of prey. It gives the strongest eaglet a better chance of surviving to adulthood. On average, more than three-quarters of young eagles do not make it past their first year.

(6) WEEKS

- ▸ Tiny feathers sprouting
- ▸ Active in exploring the nest
- ▸ Nearly as tall as their parents
- ▸ Weight: 6 pounds (2.7 kg)

(8) WEEKS

- ▸ Feathers cover bodies and wings
- ▸ Begin to tear up food on their own
- ▸ Flap wings and lift off the nest floor
- ▸ Weight: 8 pounds (3.6 kg)

—— FEATURED FAMILY ——

Look Who's Crawling

On Anticosti Island, the two bald eaglets are now three weeks old. Their fleshy legs are turning yellow and growing stronger, but the eaglets can still only crawl around the nest on bent ankles and knees. Their father has brought a fish to the nest. The eaglets instinctively poke at it, but their beaks are still too weak to function. Their mother offers a chunk of fish meat to the male eaglet. The female eaglet pushes her smaller brother out of the way and gobbles up the fleshy food. But her little brother will not give up. He pushes right back and nabs the next bit of food offered by his mother. He must fight to survive his sister's aggression.

MOST
EAGLE SPECIES HAVE
ONE TO THREE
OFFSPRING.

(9) WEEKS

- ▸ Grow stronger
- ▸ Begin branching
- ▸ Weight: 9 pounds (4.1 kg)

Eaglets are some of the fastest-growing birds on Earth. They are fed up to eight times a day and gain about a pound (0.5 kg) a week until they are full-grown. As their leg strength increases, they become curious and eager explorers. They often crawl to the edge of the nest and peek over. Eaglets have dark eyes that turn gray, golden brown, or yellow as they age. The Philippine eagle is the only bird of prey with blue eyes. Eagles have a see-through inner eyelid called a nictitating membrane. Hatchlings have poor eyesight, but it improves every day. When they reach adulthood, some eagle species have vision four or five times sharper than normal human eyesight.

—————— FEATURED FAMILY ——————

Give It a Try

A black beetle creeps over the edge of the nest. Spotting the movement, the eaglets scuttle toward it, cheeping excitedly. The male eaglet flaps his bony wings and kicks with his feet as though swimming. He falls forward, landing short of the insect. The female eaglet reaches the beetle. She instinctively opens her beak and lunges forward. But her aim is off, and the beetle escapes. It will be several months before the eaglets are ready to capture their own prey.

CLOSE-UP
Food shredders

Eagles do not chew their food. They typically shred their prey and swallow bite-sized pieces. Snake eagles, mostly found in Africa, may slurp whole snakes like strings of spaghetti!

(11) **WEEKS**

- ▸ Fly away from the nest for the first time
- ▸ Explore surroundings
- ▸ Return to the nest to be fed by parents
- ▸ Weight: 10.5 pounds (4.8 kg)

CLOSE-UP
Syrinx

Eagles do not have vocal cords. The sounds they make are produced in a bony chamber, called the syrinx, at the bottom of the throat.

CHAPTER THREE

LIFE LESSONS

By the time eaglets are about six weeks old, they have grown nearly as tall as their parents. Until they strengthen their muscles, though, eaglets this age weigh much less than their parents. They look nothing like adult eagles, either. Their down falls out in patches as new feathers begin to grow. These new feathers are called blood feathers because they are rich with blood as they grow. They are also known as pin feathers because they are about the size of pins when they first emerge. Bird feathers are hollow like drinking straws. Birds also have hollow bones, making them lightweight for flight. Growing new feathers takes a couple of weeks. Eagles continue to molt in patches throughout their lives, mostly in the summer months.

(13) WEEKS

- Fly farther from the nest
- Practice hunting on their own
- Return to the nest to sleep at night
- Weight: 12 pounds (5.4 kg)

(16) WEEKS

- Full-grown
- Leave the nest
- Share their parents' hunting area

Keeping cool

Eagles do not sweat. To cool off, they may perch in the shade or hold their wings away from their body if shade is unavailable. They also pant like dogs.

FEATURED · FAMILY

This Is How It's Done

The young eaglets on Anticosti Island have been waiting for their mother to return with food. She arrives with a small hare. But she does not feed the eaglets. Holding the carcass down with her sharp talons, she digs her razor-sharp beak into the animal's soft belly and peels back a layer of fur and skin. The eaglets watch her. Then, following her example, they drive their own beaks into the soft flesh, slicing away bits of meat. This is how it's done.

At the age of eight weeks, eaglets have strong legs and walk around the nest. They are more independent. The mated pair can leave them alone in the nest for extended periods of time. When their parents bring food to the nest, eaglets dig their talons into the meal. They use the tips of their hooked beaks to shred the meat and feed themselves. Eaglets now have full wing feathers. When gusts of wind blow through the nest, they instinctively flap their wings and lift off the nest floor. Hovering for short periods builds their muscles and helps eaglets prepare for their first flight.

When they are 9 to 10 weeks old, eaglets begin branching. This is a behavior that helps eaglets improve their balance and coordination

(3) YEARS

- Brown feathers on heads and tails are replaced with white feathers
- Now expert hunters
- Bodies are more slender
- Weight: 14.5 pounds (6.6 kg)

skills. They flap their wings and hop to the rim of the nest. Then they hop-fly to a branch next to the nest. They may do this many times until they no longer wobble or tilt. By the time eaglets are 12 weeks old, they fly away from the nest for the first time. This is called fledging, and the young birds are now known as fledglings. Some eagle species return to the nest to sleep with their parents and beg for food for up to eight more weeks. Others simply leave home to make their own way in the world.

— FEATURED FAMILY —

Practice Makes Perfect

A breeze blows up to the nest. The eaglets spread their wings, flap quickly, and rise from the nest floor, hovering for a few moments. Next, they hop-fly to the edge of the nest. It's 80 feet (24.4 m) down to the forest floor. The female eaglet flaps her wings and hop-flies to a nearby branch. She wobbles for a moment, and then settles. Her brother hop-flies to another branch. The eaglets return to the nest and rest before trying again. They will continue practicing on and off for several more days.

12 WEEKS OLD

Eaglets fly away from the nest for the **FIRST TIME.**

(4) YEARS

▸ Search for lifetime mates
▸ Nest and raise first sets of offspring

(30) YEARS

▸ End of lives

CHAPTER FOUR

EAGLE SPOTTING

Eagles around the world face many challenges. When their habitat is destroyed, they may not be able to find other places to feed and nest. When farmers and ranchers poison pesky rabbits or other small animals, eagles can die from eating the tainted meat. And when industries pollute water sources, fish often die, leaving eagles with a lack of food. Eagles living near developed areas are frequently electrocuted on power lines or struck by wind turbines. In some countries, they are hunted for food. In other places, eagles are killed because farmers wrongly believe the birds prey on their livestock.

Scientists with the Harpy Eagle Conservation Program in South America work to learn more about harpy eagles so that they can find ways to protect and preserve these birds and their habitats. The Spanish imperial eagle was once critically endangered, with only 30 breeding pairs in existence in the 1960s. But conservation efforts in Spain and Portugal have led to a tenfold increase today. When Chumphon Raptor Center opened in Thailand in 2012, it became the first facility dedicated to studying eagles and other birds of prey in all of Southeast Asia. By educating people about the ecological value of raptors, Chumphon hopes to stop people from hunting eagles for food.

Bald and golden eagles are the only eagle species in the United States and Canada. Numerous research and conservation facilities exist to support these eagles. One such place is the National Eagle Center, located on the banks of the Mississippi River in Wabasha, Minnesota. Injured bald and golden eagles are rehabilitated at the center. Some are released back into the wild. Those that can no longer survive on their own are given a safe place to stay.

Because eagles compete with humans for habitat, protected areas have been created to help eagles thrive. A natural sanctuary for bald eagles is the Alaska Chilkat Bald Eagle Preserve. This 48,000-acre (19,425 ha) preserve is located along the Chilkat, Kleheni, and Tsirku rivers. It is home to the world's largest concentration of wild bald eagles. Although eagles may appear fierce and powerful, these birds live a fragile existence. They need our understanding and support to survive in the world we share with them. Preserving and protecting our natural resources is an important step toward making the world a better place for eagles.

SNAPSHOTS

The **harpy eagle** of South America has one of the biggest wingspans of any eagle—up to 6.5 feet (2 m). At five inches (12.7 cm) long, its talons are longer than a grizzly bear's claws!

The **South Nicobar serpent eagle** is the world's smallest eagle. It grows to just 17 inches (43.2 cm) from head to tail.

Tawny eagles make loose stick nests in trees or on the ground in their woodland and grassland habitats of Africa and southwestern Asia.

The rare **black-and-chestnut eagle** lives on the forested slopes of South America's Andes Mountains at elevations of more than 5,280 feet (1,609 m).

Steller's sea-eagle is the heaviest eagle, weighing up to 20 pounds (9.1 kg). It breeds only on the eastern coast of Russia.

The **southern banded snake eagle** of East Africa uses its talons to pierce the skulls of large snakes and then shred them into bite-sized pieces.

Found only on the island of Madagascar, the rare **Madagascar serpent eagle** feeds mainly on lizards and frogs.

The feet of India and Southeast Asia's **lesser fish eagles** are specialized for walking on wet rocks. Sharp, fleshy bumps on the bottom of their toes are similar to cleats on baseball shoes.

Black eagles of tropical Asia often steal eggs and hatchlings from the nests of other birds. Sometimes they carry away entire nests!

The **golden eagle** is the second-largest eagle in North America after the **bald eagle**. It can have a wingspan of up to seven feet (2.1 m).

Bateleurs of Africa can cruise at speeds of up to 50 miles (80.5 km) per hour. Their hunting grounds can be 250 square miles (648 sq km).

African **crowned eagles** prey on animals that weigh up to four times more than they do, including monkeys and small antelopes.

Despite their name, **black solitary eagles** sometimes hunt in teams. They live in Mexico and Central and South America.

WORDS to Know

carcass the body of a dead animal

ecological having to do with the relationships of organisms living together within an environment

endangered at risk of disappearing from the Earth forever

molt to lose old feathers and grow new feathers to replace them

nictitating membrane clear tissue that sweeps across the eye from side to side to clean and protect the eye

species a group of living beings with shared characteristics and the ability to reproduce with one another

talons claws on the ends of a bird of prey's toes

thermals circular, upward-moving currents of warm air

LEARN MORE

Books

Alderfer, Jonathan. *National Geographic Kids Bird Guide of North America.* 2nd ed. Washington, D.C.: National Geographic Kids, 2018.

Burnie, David. *DK Eyewitness: Eagle & Birds of Prey.* London: DK, 2016.

Reynolds, Toby, and Paul Calver. *Birds of Prey.* Hauppauge, N.Y.: Barron's Educational Series, 2017.

Websites

"Bald Eagle." National Geographic Kids. https://kids.nationalgeographic.com /animals/bald-eagle/.

"Explore Raptors: Eagles." The Peregrine Fund. https://www.peregrinefund .org/explore-raptors-query&erqtypeIclass&erqparam=1.

"Harpy Eagle." San Diego Zoo Animals & Plants. http://animals.sandiegozoo .org/animals/harpy-eagle.

Documentaries

Landin, Bo. *Return of the Raptors.* New York: FilmRise, 2013.

Nadaskay, Istvan. *The Saga of the White-Tailed Eagle.* Vienna, Austria: ORF Universum, 2010.

Tyner, Martin, and Susan Tyner. *The Bald Eagle That Would Not Quit.* Southwest Wildlife Foundation of Utah, 2017.

Note: Every effort has been made to ensure that any websites listed above were active at the time of publication. However, because of the nature of the Internet, it is impossible to guarantee that these sites will remain active indefinitely or that their contents will not be altered.

Visit

CALEDON STATE PARK

This 2,587-acre (1,047 ha) park features guided tours to spot wild bald eagles.

11617 Caledon Road
King George, VA 22485

EAGLE MOUNTAIN SANCTUARY

This site is home to the largest group of un-releasable bald eagles in the U.S.

2700 Dollywood Parks Boulevard
Pigeon Forge, TN 37863

OWL ORPHANED WILDLIFE REHABILITATION SOCIETY

Visitors can see and learn about the resident raptors at this facility.

3800 72nd Street
Delta, BC
Canada V4K 3N2

SAN DIEGO ZOO

Several eagle species are represented in this popular zoo.

2920 Zoo Drive
San Diego, CA 92101

INDEX

beaks 9, 10, 14, 16, 20, 21
conservation measures 13, 25–26
    protected areas 25, 26
    research centers 25–26
ecological value 7, 26
eggs 4, 6, 8, 13
eyes 10, 16
feathers 6, 10, 14, 19, 21
feet 9, 14, 20, 21, 28, 29
    talons 9, 20, 21, 28
food 7, 9, 10, 13, 14, 16, 17, 20, 21, 22, 25, 28, 29

legs 14, 16, 21
mating 4, 10, 13, 21, 25, 28
movement 9, 12, 14, 16, 19, 21–22, 29
offspring 8, 9–10, 13, 14, 16, 19, 20, 21, 22
populations 13, 25, 26
species 4, 7, 8, 10, 13, 14, 16, 17, 20, 22, 25, 26, 28, 29
threats 9, 10, 12, 13, 14, 25, 26
vocalizations 4, 10, 16, 18
wings 8, 10, 16, 20, 21, 22, 28, 29